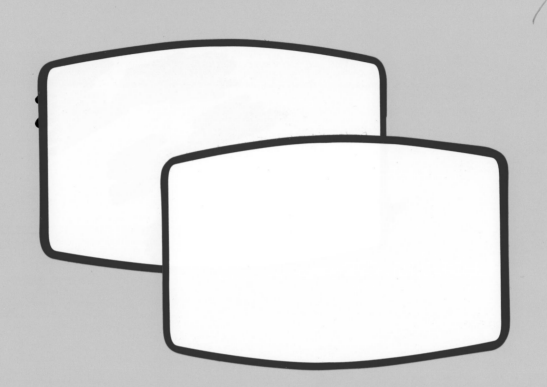

Little Dogs

INTRODUCTION BY TIM BLANKS

CHRONICLE BOOKS

SAN FRANCISCO

INCREDIBLY, INORDINATELY, DEVASTATINGLY, IMMORTALLY,
CALAMITOUSLY, HEARTENINGLY, ADORABLY BEAUTIFUL ...

Little Dogs

INTRODUCTION BY TIM BLANKS

Little dogs have rarely enjoyed a bigger profile than in these early years of the twenty-first century – and the less there is of the dog, the more there is of the media coverage. That's almost inevitable when your lot in life is to play constant companion to some of the most glamorously public women of our era. And today, it's just not enough to be a girl's best friend. A small dog must also be purebred arm candy: thin, food-averse, looks good in diamonds, and perfectly happy to make her home in the handbag of the season … why, she's the very mirror of her mistress.

This is the age of the bonsai breed, the teacup canine, dogs so tiny that vets have trouble getting pills and needles small enough to treat them when they fall ill (as such delicate constitutions frequently do). When Paris Hilton's Chihuahua Tinkerbell began to tip the scales at three pounds or more, she gave her up for the more bijou Bambi. So much for best friends, though perhaps Paris felt her own slender frame simply wasn't up to toting Tink's bulk any longer.

Paris and Tinkerbell could fairly claim credit for the attention paid to a girl and her dog in this day and age. They were inseparable at so many photo opportunities that they became an item in the tabloid press. Any number of publicity-hungry starlets-on-the-make took this as a cue, and now no red carpet is complete without a sliver of starlet clutching a petite morsel of dog. It's exactly the same backstage at fashion shows, but that's Gisele Bündchen's fault. Before she became Leonardo diCaprio's squeeze, the Brazilian bombshell was as one with Vida, her Yorkshire terrier. Even now, she insists her life-savers on a desert island would be her dog, her man and her perfume – in that order.

So what is it with beautiful women and small dogs? It's scarcely a new thing. The love of Jean Harlow's life was her Pomeranian. Audrey Hepburn was fiercely attached to her Yorkie, Mr. Famous. Elizabeth Taylor's recently deceased Maltese terrier Sugar will go down in history as the longest-lasting of her partners. You could probably make a good case for women like these feeling somewhat jaundiced about human company. Beauty, after all, has a habit of eventually, inevitably offering an illusion-free lens through which to view the baser motivations of mankind. So a tiny, vulnerable, lovable (and unconditionally loving) creature would seem like a sweet – and discreet – anodyne.

Jackie Kennedy may have had her German shepherd, Marilyn Monroe her basset hound, but it's an inescapable truth that the most favoured breeds – Lhasa apsos, Pekingese, pugs – have flat little faces which tend to make their eyes look larger and more childlike, all the better to suggest an innately empathetic nature. The tiny heads of the pointy-faced terrier types – the Chihuahuas, Yorkies, dachshunds and Maltese – turn their eyes into saucers too. And, significantly, all of these dogs stay puppy-sized for the duration of their usually long lives.

Any doting dog-lover has fielded comments about child substitutes. Knowing what we now know about the relationships many stars "enjoyed" with their offspring, it's no wonder someone as image-conscious as Joan Crawford preferred to step out with her dog Clicquot (his tiny outfits tailored to match hers) rather than her scheming minx of a daughter. You can say whatever you like about such a couple being perfectly in tune with the terminal narcissism the entertainment industry requires of its players (and Joan was undoubtedly one narcissistic link in a chain that runs all the way up to Paris and her pals), but given the children and husbands Crawford was blessed with, it's surprising she didn't enlist a whole lot more Clicquots to function as a family substitute.

That was certainly the course of action adopted by the legendary art collecting millionairess Peggy Guggenheim, husbands and daughter notwithstanding. She lies buried in the grounds of her Venetian palazzo, surrounded by the graves of her fourteen Lhasas. Same with the Duchess of Windsor. She and her Duke surrounded themselves with a court of pugs, an imperial lapdog if ever there was one. Their little courtiers ate out of solid silver bowls, and lived amongst the Windsors' large collection of puggery – priceless Meissen figurines, elaborately framed "family" portraits. The Duke's niece Elizabeth prefers corgis to pugs – and possibly also prefers them to her own litter of wayward Windsors.

But blue blood is no prerequisite to sharing the sentiments of the Queen. A survey of women over twenty-five found that a *substantial* majority thought dogs were more affectionate, more easygoing, more loyal and more reliable than men – 75 percent turned to their dogs for succour when they felt down.

On the other hand, some anonymous number-cruncher came to the conclusion that you are three times more likely to meet someone to become romantically involved with when you are with a dog. It could, of course, be a plot on the part of the canny canine. On a walk in the park, set up a yearning single with her prince charming, sit back with a bone – and watch the whole thing go horribly wrong. And whose shoulder will the broken heart cry on?

Tim Blanks

The Ultimate Accessory

Dog, n. A kind of

designed to catch the overflow and

additional or subsidiary Deity

surplus of the world's worship.

My little dog – a heartbeat at my feet.

Edith Wharton

All in the town were still asleep,

When the sun came up with a shout and a leap.

In the lonely streets unseen by man,

A *little dog* danced. And the day began.

"The Little Dog's Day", Rupert Brooke

Maybe I was *born to play ball*. Maybe I truly was.

Willie Mays

Pooch Perfect Spa Escapes

These resorts have truly gone to the dogs! Tucked away inside the soothing surroundings of a world-class spa, a pampered guest has just enjoyed a relaxing bath followed by a deep tissue massage, and is now receiving a pedicure . . . on all four feet. Yes, it's true – spa resorts have finally gone to the dogs, and our canine companions couldn't be happier! After all, isn't it about time Fido got his own masseuse and late night room service? And what dog wouldn't drool over a chef-prepared gourmet menu and handmade turndown treats?

Heather Davis, *Fido Friendly Magazine*

33% of pet owners are reputed to talk to their pets
on the phone or through the answering machine.

The dog is the god of frolic.

Walt Whitman

Money will buy you a fine dog,
but only love can make it wag its tail.

Richard Friedman

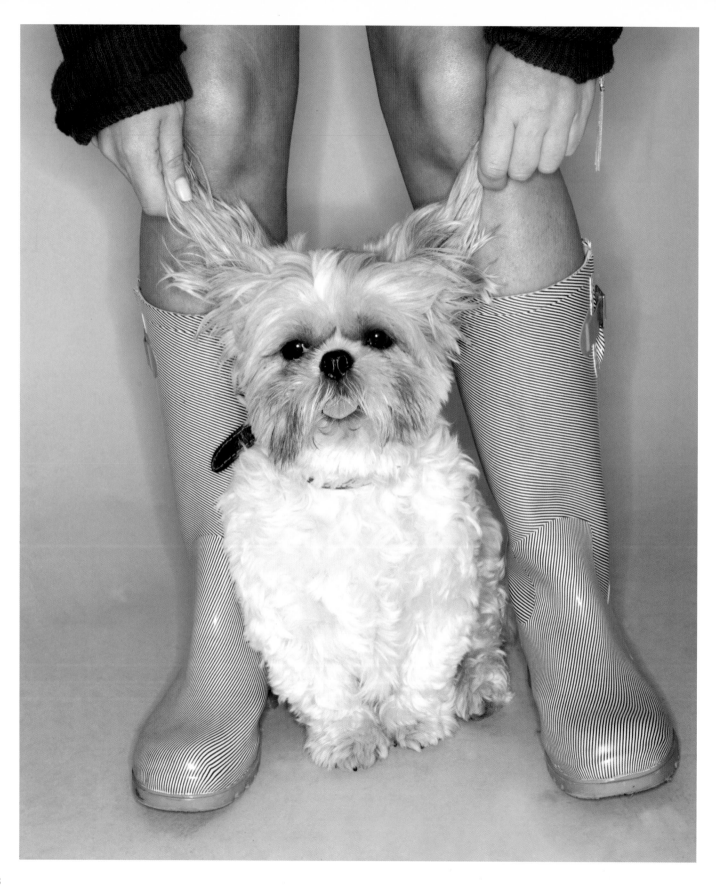

I hope *if dogs take over the world,* and they choose a king, they don't just go by size, because I bet there are some Chihuahuas with some good ideas.

Jack Handey

Did you ever notice when you blow
But when you take him in a car

in a dog's face he gets mad at you?
he sticks his head out the window.

Steve Bluestone

How beautiful it is to do nothing,
and then to rest afterward.

Spanish proverb

Yesterday I was a dog. Today I'm a dog. *Sigh!* There's so little

Tomorrow I'll probably still be a dog.

hope for advancement. Charles M. Schulz

The more mischief, the better the sport.

Scottish proverb

World's smallest dog ...

the smallest dog in history was reputedly a tiny Yorkie from Blackburn, England. At two years of age and fully grown, this little dog was an incredible 2.5 inches tall by 3.75 inches long. He weighed only 4 ounces and was approximately the size of a matchbox.

I know that dogs are pack animals, but it is difficult to imagine a pack of poodles ... And if there was such a thing as a pack of poodles, where would they rove to?

Bloomingdale's?

Yvonne Clifford

The most *affectionate* creature in the world is a *wet dog*.

Ambrose Bierce

If you think dogs can't count,
try putting three dog biscuits in your pocket and
then giving Fido only two of them.

Phil Pastoret

Dachshunds are ideal dogs for small children, as they are already stretched and pulled to such a length that the child cannot do much harm one way or the other.

Robert Benchley

Never wear anything that panics the cat.

P. J. O'Rourke

This dog is having a hard time choosing between a mink coat, a diamond collar and a leather sports coat at the Swank Poodletown shop on New York's Park Avenue.

Circa 1956

It's Hard to Leash a Dog Owner Once Bitten by Fashion Bug

Time was when all a dog wore was a collar. Nowadays, however, the coddled canine may turn up at the beach in a bikini or at a party in false eyelashes.

There are plain coats, raincoats and mink coats, to protect him from the elements. With Happy Breath he needn't worry about offending his friends. And for that really big occasion, when everybody is putting on the dog, he might just show up in a set of glue-on toenails.

"Everybody wants their dog to look different these days", said Jack Irving, who sells dogs and dog togs at Schnauzers Only, Inc., … "Take a good look at them [dogs] sometime," he added, "and all you'll see are rhinestones and silly doo-dads."

New York Times

Energy and persistence conquer all things.

Benjamin Franklin

You may have a dog that won't sit up,
not because she's too stupid to learn how

roll over or even cook breakfast,

but because she's too smart to bother.

Rick Horowitz

Audrey Hepburn was accompanied everywhere by her Yorkshire terrier *Famous* who lived up to his name with walk-on roles in some of her films.

You are three times

become romantically

more likely to meet someone to
involved with when you are with a dog.

Sugar & spice and all things nice.

Nursery rhyme

From *a dog's point of view* his master is an
elongated and abnormally cunning dog.

Mabel L. Robinson

I soon learned that having a show dog is like having a kid in boarding school. You are constantly required to send money and equipment, but you rarely see your offspring. When she comes home she usually needs grooming and she claims not to know who you are. She wants to parade around the kitchen and be applauded. She doesn't want to mess up her coiffure by wrestling with you on the floor or muck up her smile fetching sticks. She is, in short, a snob.

"A Woman's Best Friend", Erica Jong, *Cigar Aficionado*

Fashions fade, style is eternal.

Yves Saint Laurent

Not *Carnegie, Vanderbilt* raised money enough to buy

and *Astor* together could have
a quarter–share in my little dog. Ernest Thompson Seton

Money spent annually in America on dog accessories, 1959 estimate:

US $150,000,000.00

Backstage... at last month's John Galliano show, the models, stylists and make-up artists had to contend with what seemed like a small pack of toy dogs. There was yapping and snarling and demands for more attention – all of which meant (drum roll and cymbal, please) that the canines fitted right in: it was a clear illustration of the natural sympathy between small dog and model that is making the former such a fashionable, four-legged accessory. Minimutt-ism, we like to call it; it takes in all-comers from Japanese chin to Yorkshire terrier, but its star is the shih-tzu.

Richard Benson, the *Guardian*

The little dog laughed to see such sport.

Nursery rhyme

She was such a *beautiful and sweet creature* ... and so full of tricks.

Queen Victoria, on her dachshund

Anyone can catch your eye, but it takes
someone special to catch your heart.

'Tis pity not to have a dog, whatever be his breed,

for dogs possess a faithfulness, which humans sadly need.

And whether skies be blue or gray, good luck or ill attend

Man's toil by day, a dog will stay, his ever-constant friend.

"A Dog", Edgar A. Guest

No one appreciates the very *special genius* of your conversation as a dog does.

Christopher Morley

I awoke one morning and found myself famous.

Lord Byron

He never chooses an opinion;
he just wears whatever happens to be in style.

Leo Tolstoy

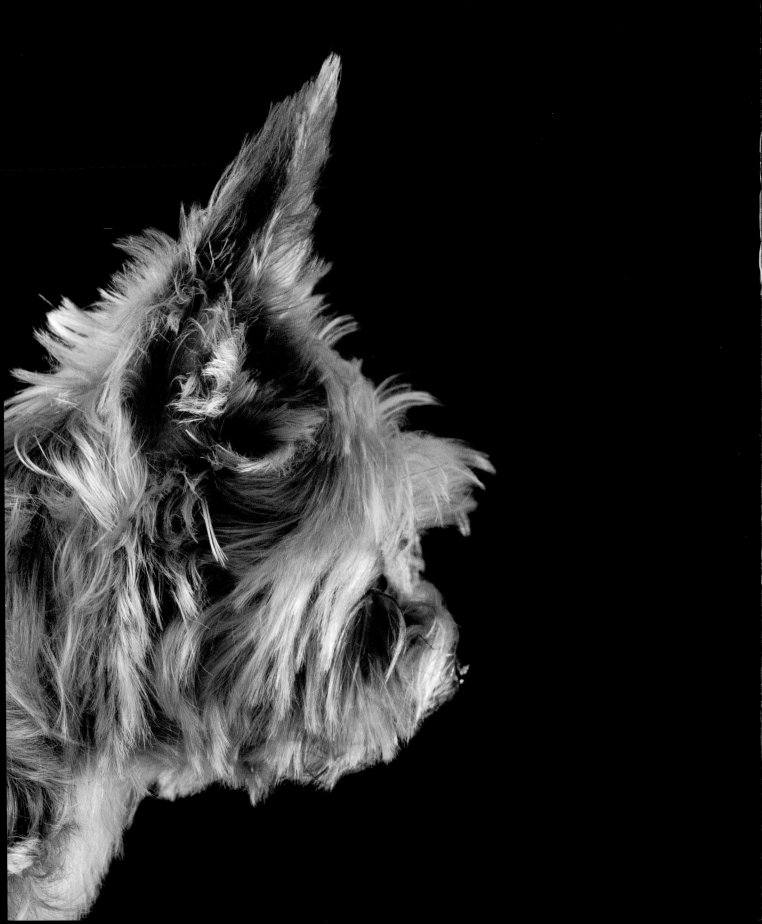

I am I because my little dog knows me.

Gertrude Stein

One's style is one's signature always.

Oscar Wilde

Dog Horoscopes

virgo: Mercury is the ruling planet of Virgo. Mercury's influence varies in intensity, but strongly affects your internal wellbeing. So while you love luxury, be careful of your tummy, since it is very delicate … Your romantic life will be a busy whirlwind, but don't rush into a hasty relationship! According to the stars your best relationship would be with one born between December 22 and January 19. Your favorite color is orange. *August 24 – September 23*

libra: You are resourceful and clever, but your retrieving skills leave something to be desired. You probably have the nickname One Way Retriever (even if you aren't a retriever) since you show great enthusiasm going after a ball but getting you (and the ball) to come back can be a real challenge … Be careful of your back and don't take too many tumbles. Your lucky number is 6 and your most favorite color is turquoise.
September 24 – October 23

scorpio: You were born under the Sign of the Scorpio, which symbolizes your strength, determination and makes you a natural leader. In addition you are a proficient swimmer, unless of course you have just had your hair done or someone has had the nerve to throw you into the swimming pool at a wild party … You can be ruthless like the eagle and will go through any ordeal for your loved ones. Watch your paws carefully, stay away from drafts and never indulge in rich foods. *October 24 – November 22*

sagittarius: You are a natural born hunter and will stalk anything that moves including ants, butterflies, and old newspapers … You have a very passionate temperament and are sensitive and sympathetic to the moods of those around you … Harsh words or tone of voice will cause you resentment and you will pretend not to understand. A bath is revolting and so are cats. *November 23 – December 22*

capricorn: The Goat symbolizes the ability to scale heights and this will be your driving force since you are the ultimate social climber. You adore trips to the doggy salon and "beautiful dog of the year" is your greatest desire. You just intuitively know that the nicer you appear to others the more likely you are to get what you want … And, you are such a FLIRT. Roll those eyes, wag that tail and you have the attention of everyone in the park! *December 23 – January 20*

aquarius: You are intuitive, handsome, very friendly towards everyone, but devoted to your family. While you may seem uninterested in what is going on around you, you are thrilled when someone fusses over you. Those that really know and understand you always have a treat for you … In the area of love you have roving eyes and a tail wagging welcome! Your favorite color is vibrant electric blue. Your desire for rainy weather may be hard to satisfy. *January 21 – February 19* *pisces:* You are highly sensitive to others and shrink away from an "apparently" friendly person because you "know" something is not right. Your howling may indicate your awareness of pending peril. And when you appear to bark "at nothing" those around you should be on guard. When you sense good, you are gentle and unassuming, and love being scratched around your ears and tummy. *February 20 – March 20*

aries: ME FIRST! That's you! Aries is the first sign of the Zodiac; the sign of a born leader. Your natural vitality drives you to be the "lead dog" and to stay the "lead dog". You fall in love at first sight and first sight will mean a sweetheart on every corner. Left alone in these situations (even momentarily) could result in an unexpected litter of Look-a-Like-Me's. Work on being less stubborn and more flexible (if only you could!). *March 21 – April 20*

taurus: Your greatest fault (I know you didn't think you had any) is your inability to get along peacefully with other dogs. Your nervous energy sets the tone and the turf war begins. Distance should be your mantra ... But your greatest love is your love of singing (well not everyone calls it that!). Your early attempts will surprise some, but once encouraged your talent grows. And you don't wait for a full moon either; radio, TV, someone humming, a group of revelers or carolers and you instantly become engaged. *April 21 – May 21*

gemini: Your aim in life is to find as many outlets as possible for your exuberant nature. Your unusually high intelligence demands a constant need for change in your environment ... A very happy and productive year lies ahead. There will be much going on in the home and there is also the possibility of two offers for your paw in marriage ... But because you are of a dual nature (The Twins), you are forever changing your mind and will probably reject both offers. *May 22 – June 21*

cancer: You have regal and engaging qualities if you want to use them. But your friends think you are too proud and arrogant (although it is usually a sign, a secret sign, of your love) ... With the Moon as your guide you are the ultimate romantic and you are the eternal optimist. You never get discouraged and this makes you a cherished companion since you are able to cheer up your dear ones ... Maintain a simple and healthful diet since your digestion and gastric troubles must be watched carefully. *June 22 – July 23*

leo: Leo is the sign of the ruler or commander – you are also known as "The King of Dogs". A courageous watchdog, you can be fierce if necessary, but if truth be told you like children and are mischievous. As long as you feel secure in your kingdom you will not run off and join the circus (although you are a natural born comedian who enjoys entertaining). Don't be so afraid of thunder or lightning. Sunbathe on beautiful mornings. *July 24 – August 23*

Mystic Dog

It is impossible to overdo *luxury*.

French proverb

If you don't own a dog, at least anything wrong with you, but there may

one, there is not necessarily
be something wrong with your life.

Roger Caras

Life is an endless struggle full of frustrations and challenges,
but eventually you find a hair style you like.

No matter how little money and how few possessions
you own, having a dog makes you *rich*.

Louis Sabin

Love me, love my dog.

Latin proverb

Acknowledgements

Photographic credits
All photographs in this book, including the cover, are Getty Images except for the following:
p. 35 Herbert Spichtinger/zefa/Corbis; p. 67 Photolibrary; p. 103 Chris Collins/Corbis; p. 115 PQ Blackwell;
p. 124 Pat Doyle/Corbis.

Further text attributions
The quotation "Incredibly, inordinately, devastatingly, immortally, calamitously, hearteningly, adorably beautiful" which
appears on the cover and on the title page is by Rupert Brooke; the quotation on p. 10 is by Ambrose Bierce; the statistic on
p. 28 is from a study by the American Animal Hospital Association; quotations on p. 112 and p. 142 are by an unknown
source.

The publisher would like to thank Getty Images for their help in compiling the imagery in this book.

First published in the United States in 2007 by Chronicle Books LLC.

Copyright © 2007 by PQ Blackwell Limited

Library of Congress Cataloging-in-Publication Data is available.

ISBN-10: 0-8118-5833-2
ISBN-13: 978-0-8118-5833-5

Manufactured in China

Designed by Carolyn Lewis and Cameron Gibb
PQ Blackwell Limited, 116 Symonds Street, Auckland, New Zealand

Distributed in Canada by Raincoast Books
9050 Shaughnessy Street
Vancouver, British Columbia V6P 6E5

10 9 8 7 6 5 4 3 2 1

Chronicle Books LLC
680 Second Street
San Francisco, California 94107
www.chroniclebooks.com

The publisher is grateful for literary permissions to reproduce those items below subject to copyright. Every effort has been made to trace the copyright holders and the publisher apologizes for any unintentional omission. We would be pleased to hear from any not acknowledged here and undertake to make all reasonable efforts to include the appropriate acknowledgements in any subsequent editions.

"Pooch Perfect Spa Escapes" on p. 26 reprinted with permission of Heather Davis; quotation on p. 36 reprinted with permission of Richard Friedman; quotation on p. 40 from *Deep Thoughts*, copyright © 1992 by Jack Handey, used by permission of Berkley Publishing Group, a division of Penguin Group (USA) Inc.; quotation on p. 42 reprinted with permission of Steve Bluestone; quotation on p. 50 reprinted with permission of Peanuts/United Media; quotation on p. 77 copyright © 1967 by The New York Times Co. reprinted with permission; quotation on p. 83 reprinted with permission of Rick Horowitz; excerpt on p. 96 reprinted with permission of Erica Jong; dog horoscopes on p. 132 reprinted with permission of www.doghoroscopes.com; quotation on p. 138 reprinted with permission of Jill and Pamela Caras.